HINDUISM:
DAWNING OF FIRST LIGHT OF A DEVOTEE

Poonam Kukreja

PARTRIDGE

Copyright © 2023 by Poonam Kukreja.

| ISBN: | Softcover | 978-1-5437-7413-9 |
| | eBook | 978-1-5437-7412-2 |

All rights reserved. No part of this book may be used or reproduced by any means, graphic, electronic, or mechanical, including photocopying, recording, taping or by any information storage retrieval system without the written permission of the author except in the case of brief quotations embodied in critical articles and reviews.

Because of the dynamic nature of the Internet, any web addresses or links contained in this book may have changed since publication and may no longer be valid. The views expressed in this work are solely those of the author and do not necessarily reflect the views of the publisher, and the publisher hereby disclaims any responsibility for them.

Print information available on the last page.

To order additional copies of this book, contact
Toll Free +65 3165 7531 (Singapore)
Toll Free +60 3 3099 4412 (Malaysia)
orders.singapore@partridgepublishing.com

www.partridgepublishing.com/singapore

Contents

Preface	vii
Temple Worship	1
Deities - Symbolisms	3
Brahma	4
Saraswati	6
Vishnu	8
Lakshmi	10
Shiva	12
Parvati – Goddess of Strength and Protection	15
Ganesha - Remover of Obstacle	17
Vibhuti (Vibhooti)	19
The Rudraksha	19
Navarathri	21
Kolam/Rangoli	23
Deepavali / Diwali Celebrations	25
Two Great Epics of Hinduism	27
The Ramayana	28
The Mahabharata	30
A Hindu Marriage - Saptapadi - The Marriage Vows	32
The Search For Peace	36
What Are Desires	40
Vegetarianism	44
Meditation	46

Preface

This book is for the inquiring mind to know what the Hindu religion is about. At every point of one's life, many questions and enquiries would visit the mind. What is life, what is religion and what is my role. How does one fit into the system as a well accomplished human being. This book would serve as a starting point for inquiring and understanding the Hindu religion.

Poonam Kukreja

SIGNIFICANCE OF THE HINDU RITUALS

Temple Worship

Rituals:- Rituals are the external way of worship by a devotee who is progressing on the path of God. It is a great truth that whatever external worship is performed during prayer, has a significance for the devotee's inner development.

Bathing the Idols:- *Abishegam* shows the devotee that his external physical body should be kept clean, likewise his internal self by pure love and devotion. Bathing the Idol with milk, curd, ghee and 5 nectars, shows that as the body is made to feel beautiful and healthy, thus the mind must also grow beautiful and good by feeding it with good thoughts.

Dressing Idols:- By dressing the Idols with beautiful garments, the devotee personifies the beauty of God. In doing this the devotee feels happy.

Garlands & Singing:- In offering garlands and singing beautiful songs of praise, the devotee feels that he is entertaining a great person and he feels greatly honoured and happy.

Curtain in front of Idol:- The curtain represents the veil of ignorance that hides the inner vision of God. In addition, we must get rid of all negative qualities in us so as to see the truth which is within us.

Lamps:- It indicates that the one God gives life to the innumerable beings on earth. By lighting the lamp, it signifies the path of truth and righteousness.

<u>Burning of Camphor:-</u> When praying, we light the camphor to ask God, "I am showing this light before you, please let me see you. Put me on the path of brightness to gain knowledge and remove the ignorance in me". *Maya* is ignorance and darkness. Thus devotees pray, "Dear God, please remove maya and give me the light of True Knowledge."

<u>Breaking of Coconut:-</u> The devotee is asking God, "Please break my hard ego/pride (coconut shell) and fill me with love and purity (coconut water). Help me to be clean and white as the coconut kernel (purity). Here the devotee vows to break whatever ego/pride in oneself.

<u>The Bell:-</u> The Bell represents the source of the Primal Cosmic Sound-*OMKARA*. The auspicious sound of the bell will invite the devas to our pooja and drive away any evil forces that maybe present. Once the bell is rung, our concentration should divert into the prayers fully.

ॐ

What do the deities we see everyday and pray to symbolise?

What teachings are the deities conveying to us?

Symbolism has been evolved to explain the attributes and qualities of God-head. Different iconographical features are depicted for the different deities at different times, depending on the roles they perform. A few of the major depictions are given to enable us to understand what each deity symbolises in its silent self.

The symbols and God forms were conveyed to sages in deep meditation so as to transcend the barrier of language. Once, one understands the meaning the symbols convey, language is unnecessary. The symbols convey the message, teachings and nature of Divinity.

Brahma - Creator of the Universe

Brahma the Creator, with four heads facing all four directions symbolises the great primal TRUTH and that one can approach God from any path, any direction ie religious, practice and one will be received. The Vedas he holds in his hand (the leaf parchment) tell us that creation is closely associated with knowledge and this is the creative power, god has gifted to man. He sits on a lotus which is a symbol of purity. The lotus usually grows in muddy waters but is untouched by the dirt and mire from which it emerges. Likewise if one wishes Divinity to manifest in one, than one should, while living within the dirt of society, be untouched and unaffected by its negativity.

Brahma also holds a *mala*(rosary) in one hand. This symbolises that man can remove the dirt (mala or mel) of negativity in one's mind by constantly chanting the name of God. The *Kamandalu* (water pot) that he holds, depicts the source of Creation/life as emerging from water.

One of the reasons why Brahma is not worshipped by man is because of the fact that the purpose of birth is to get out of the cycle of birth and death- so "creation" (to be reborn) is not desired. However since knowledge is also a creative power (and is desirable), Brahma's aspect of knowledge as symbolised by Saraswathi is propitiated.

Brahma - Creator of the Universe

Saraswati - Goddess of Knowledge and Wisdom

Saraswati the consort of Brahma, is the embodiment of learning and wisdom. In her hands she holds the *vina,* symbolising the harmony and rhythm of the Universe. The *mala* (beads) in her fingers bring out the importance of prayer and meditation to remove negativity. The palm leaf parchments represent learning and wisdom without which man is nothing.

Her saree always being white is to remind us that all knowledge of value should be pristine pure and unsullied by untruth. She sits either on the pure lotus or on a swan. The graceful swan, her vehicle, symbolises purity (white) and reminds us to separate the chaff from the grain of true knowledge, just as the swan removes the water from milk before consuming the latter.

Saraswati - Goddess of Knowledge and Wisdom

Vishnu - Preservative Aspect of Divinity

Vishnu is represented as lying on the many-headed cobra, *Ananta,* in the ocean of milk. Ananta denotes cosmic energy and the ocean symbolises *ananda* as the endless bliss and grace of the Brahman, Vishnu is given the colour blue to symbolise Infinity, as he is limitless as the blue sky. He holds the *chakra* or discuss in one hand denoting that he maintains *Dharma* (righteousness) and order in the Universe. It also denotes the Wheel of Time- the destruction aspect of Divinity. The *Shankha* or conch that he holds represents sound vibrations from the force of Creation. The *gada* or mace is for removing the evil in the world ie the royal symbol of Protection/Preservation and the lotus is the symbol of the beauty and purity of the Cosmic Universe. The vehicle of Vishnu is *Garuda*, the man-eagle, a figure of great strength, power and piety.

Vishnu - Preservative Aspect of Divinity

Lakshmi - Goddess of Prosperity

Lakshmi the consort of Vishnu, is personified as one who brings Prosperity. In one hand she holds in the *abhaya mudra* (with the hand held open with the palm facing the devotee and the fingers facing upwards) which says "Do not fear", and the other in the *varada mudra* (with the hand and palm facing the devotee but with the fingers facing downwards) a symbol of prosperity and grace she gives to the human race and a reminder to man to surrender to the feet of the Lord ie to have humility. She sits on the lotus and holds lotus flowers in her hand emphasising the importance of pure living without which her grace and giving are meaningless and prosperity but an empty shell.

Lakshmi - Goddess of Prosperity

Shiva - Destructive Aspect of Divinity

Shiva is often shown as *Nataraja*, the king of Dancers, his dance depicting the dynamic movement of Cosmic Energy. He dances on the demon, *Apasmara Purusha*, who represents our ego. In one hand Shiva holds a deer which denotes man's unsteady mind which darts hither and thither like the deer, which has to be brought under control. In another hand he holds the *damaru* (drum), the symbol of creative activity. The third hand, fire, the symbol of destruction. His fourth hand in the *abhaya mudra* which means, "Do not fear. I shall protect as I destroy". The circle of fire around him symbolises the continuity and eternal motion of the Universe through the paths of Creation, Preservation and Destruction. The River Ganga, on the head denotes divine knowledge and purity.

The crescent moon reminds us of the waxing and waning of the Moon and the movement of Time. The cobra coiling around him is, again, the symbol of Cosmic Energy. Shiva's garland of skulls reminds man that God should be propitiated to destroy the *asuras* (evil) in man. His third eye depicts that God is all-seeing and wise; placed in the centre of the forehead on which Shiva concentrates while in meditation, this spot is symbolic of the seat of wisdom. Shiva opens his third eye to destroy evil.

On the right ear, Shiva wears a *Kundala* (a jewel worn by men) and on his left ear a *tatanka* (ear ornament worn by women). This is to tell us that he is *Ardhanarishwara*, half-man and half-woman (as Parvati, his consort, is part of Shiva himself), symbolising the ideal union of man and woman. As fire and heat are inseparable, so are Shiva and Parvati one, and *purusha* (spirit) and *prakriti* (matter) are combined in them.

The ashes smeared on Shiva tell us that the body is transient and ends in ashes. The tiger-skin that he wears around his waist is the *ahamkara* or arrogant pride which, like the tiger, springs out of us and has to be suppressed. Shiva not only destroys the Universe but is also the destroyer of man's illusions, and the cycle of birth and death which binds us to this world.

Soon after the creation of this world, Shiva is believed to have appeared in the form of a pillar of fire, reaching into space at one end and into the bowels of the earth at the other (the puranic story Brahma and Vishnu are relevant here). Therefore Shiva is Symbolised as a Linga or Lingam (meaning symbol) representing this endless pillar of cosmic power and light.

He is also worshipped as Lingodbhavamurti, in which the figure of Shiva emerges out of the pillar of fire, with Brahma and Vishnu standing either side.

In all Shiva temples, his vehicle, *Nandi* the bull, faces the figure of Shiva symbolising the soul of man, the *Jiva*, yearning for *Paramatma*, the Great Soul (God).

Shiva - Destructive Aspect of Divinity

Nandi - Vehicle of Shiva

Parvati – Goddess of Strength and Protection

Cosmic Energy in its dynamic form is symbolised for us ordinary mortals in the form of *Shakti*, the World Mother, who is the power and energy by which the Great God creates, preserves and destroys the world. She is shown in many forms. As Uma or Parvati, she is the gentle consort of Shiva. As Kamashi or Rajarajeshwari, she is the Great Mother. In one hand she holds a noose or *Pasha* (rope of Love) indicating God's yearning to bind man in the rope of Love- the symbol of *Bhakti marga* (path of Devotion). The goad in her other hand is indicative of her prodding us on to the path of righteousness. The sugarcane plant she carries is a symbol of the sweetness of the Mind. The arrows she holds in one hand are our five sense-perceptions which we have to conquer. In the form of Durga she rides the tiger, the ego and arrogance that Man has to subdue. With the weapons in her hand she fights the eight evils (hate, greed, passion, vanity, contempt of others, envy, jealousy and the illusions with which man binds himself). In her angry form she is known as *Kali*, the personification of Time/Destruction. In this frightening form she destroys *Mahishasura* (the demon Buffalo) who is the symbol of ignorance which is man's greatest enemy. Her arms and weapons are constantly flaying and fighting evil in all forms. The skulls she wears tell you of the great battle man must invoke within himself to destroy the *asuras* (demonic qualities) within and neutralise them as a victory garland. Her dark form is symbolic of the future which is beyond our knowledge, and as Kali she tells you that *kala* (Time) is immutable and all-powerful in the Universe.

Parvati – Goddess of Strength and Protection
Consort of Shiva

Ganesha - Remover of Obstacle

Ganesha, also known as *Ganapati* or *Vinayaka*, is the son of Shiva and Parvati, and is the first deity to be worshipped during any ritual, as he is considered the remover of obstacles. His huge body represents the Cosmos or Universe and his trunk the *Pranava* or OM, the symbol of the Brahman. His elephant's head denotes superior intelligence and the snake around his waist represents cosmic energy. The noose is to remind us that God yearns to bind man in His rope of Love- but man has to approach God in Love (*Bhakti*) to be so bound. The goad in his hand is to prod Man on to the path of righteousness. The rosary beads are for the pursuit of prayer and the broken tusk is symbolic of sacrifice. Sage Vyasa invoked the power of the intellect-symbolised by Ganesha when he wrote the Mahabharata. The *modaka* or sweet in his hand is to remind us of the sweetness of one's inner self. The physical form of Ganesha is corpulent and awkward to teach us that beauty of the outward form has no connection with inner beauty or spiritual perfection. Ganesha, on his vehicle, the mouse, symbolises the equal importance of the biggest and the smallest of creatures to the Great God-ie the oneness of the Atma (soul).

Kartikeya

Kartikeya is the other son of Shiva. He is also known as Kumara, Skanda, Subramanya, Shanmukha or Muruga (the last name used in Tamil Nadu). As Kartikeya he is designated the deity of war, guarding right and destroying evil. As Shanmukha, the six-headed, he teaches that we have five senses and the mind, and only when all six are in harmony is there spiritual growth. As Subramanya he has two consorts, Valli and Devasena, who embody *Jnana Shakti*, the power of knowledge and *Kriya Shakti*, the power of action. He rides the peacock, reminding us not to let pride and egotism get the better of us. In his hand he holds the *vel* or sharp spear, symbolising the sharpness, broadness and depth of Knowledge that the mind must develop to become an instrument of salvation, and with it he guards the spiritual progress of the world.

Ganesha   Kartikeya

Vibhuti (Vibhooti) - (Sacred Ash or Earth)

Vibhuti- the sacred ash, has the profound symbolic duty of reminding us and society of the reality that all beings ultimately turn to ash or earth (dust). Everyone can apply vibhuti irrespective of caste, creed or religion.

Vibhuti indicates *Kaala* (time) that everything in time is ash/dust. It reminds us to make efforts to reach *Kaalaatteeta* (Lord Siva, the Lord beyond Time). The profound symbolism reminds us that all created beings turn to ash. Saint Ganasambandha says that sacred ash is the true form of Lord Siva. The same is expressed by Sage Thayumanavar- when a disciple asked, "How to attain Salvation?", he was told to always think of death. It would make the mind one pointed and help to attain the goal.

The smearing of sacred ash reminds us of a great principle, whether one is a prince or pauper, one has to end up as a handful of ash or dust/earth. So the wearing of Vibhuti emphasises the reality of the self and the transcience of the world and it's object. It reminds one to use time/life usefully.

The Rudraksha - (Prayer Beads)

Ardent devotees of *Lord Siva*, wear *Rudrakshamala*. It is used for counting their *mantra* (prayer). The number of beads on the string varies according to the way it is worn. *Sadhus* wear 3 beads on each ear, 12 beads on each wrist, 36 over the crown of the head, 32 or 72 lightly round the neck, 108 when worn as a garland. This form of *mala* (bead) is used for counting the repitition of a mantra.

The use of a mala of 27 beads gives special potency to mantra. The beads are the seeds of the rudraksha tree which grows in the Himalayas. The word mala also refers to dirt. It signifies that by chanting mantra, one removes the dirt of ignorance.

<u>The seeds can be of 4 colours</u>:
    a) White- most highly prized (rare variety)
    b) Reddish- common
    c) Golden- rare variety
    d) Dark

Navarathri

The word *Navarathri* literally translated means nine nights. This period is observed in the month of *Purattassi* starting from the new moon.

During the first three nights, *Mother Durga*, the personification of power or force is adored. This is a period of inner struggle for the aspirant who makes an attempt to transform the tainted power and energy in the self by erasing vices, impurities, weaknesses and defects by way of adoring the gracious Mother- aspect of the universal spirit with fasting, prayer session and abstinence from desires of the flesh. The request made by the aspirant is to save him from the pitfalls and dangers that blemish the soul.

During the next three nights, the aspirant, having prayed to get rid of all his negativity, aims at developing and cultivating auspicious qualities such as purity, serenity and steady effort which helps bloom forth the beauty of the *atma* (soul). This is *Deiva Sampati* (Divine Wealth). Therefore, Lakshmi does not only mean material wealth like gold, property etc. The cultivation of the above mentioned qualities in the course of time will bless the individual with self satisfaction, the greatest wealth on earth, as well as the ability to provide comfort and solace to others.

The aspirant once having routed out all evil and having cultivated pure qualities, becomes the *Adhikari* (lord). He achieves the ability to govern himself as controller and director of his senses. He is now ready to receive the light of Supreme Wisdom portrayed in the form of Sarawasti.

The tenth day is called *Vijayadasami*. *Vijaya* means Victory and *Dasami* means Tenth. *Vijayadasami* denotes the victory of the aspirant over his egoistic self and once having attained it, the Divine Knowledge, descends into him by the Grace of the Divine Mother. This day is a celebration of the victory attained by the individual soul after nine long days of austere observance.

(This period of the year is subjected to certain planetary conjunction which could affect the human psyche and mind adversely. It is recommended that we observe certain austerities during this period-fasting according to one's ability, prayers and not giving in to sensual and negative tendencies).

Kolam/Rangoli

Decorative designs of rice grains or paste drawn at the doorway to the home are generally called *Kolam* by South Indians or *Rangoli* by North Indians.

This art form is believed to have started in the Vedic period. In those days, the daily ritual of the women began with a bath, cleaning of the home, beautifying and invoking the Goddess of Prosperity, Lakshmi, at the doorway with the Kolam/Rangoli, prayer and only than she would continue with the daily household chores. The men leave the home for work only after the Kolam had been drawn.

This art form is also an expression of the yearning of housewives to perform selfless service. Whereas the menfolk could go out and serve, the women were confined to their homes where they learn to make their homes a temple of peace and harmony. The Kolam/Rangoli designs made of rice, flour etc not only lent beauty to the surroundings but served a higher purpose of feeding the insects and birds as a manifestation of their devotion to serve the Lord through His Creations.

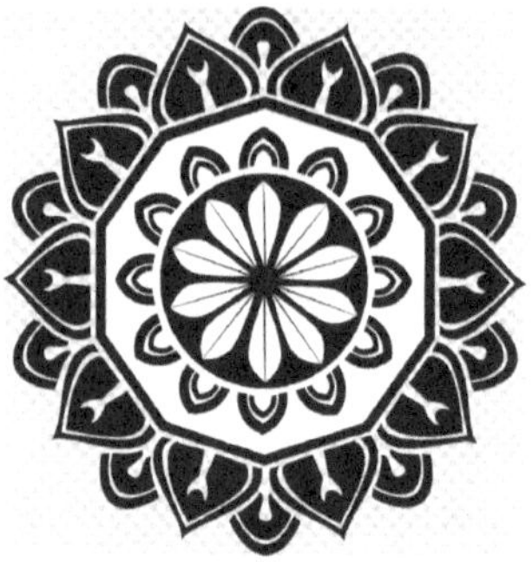
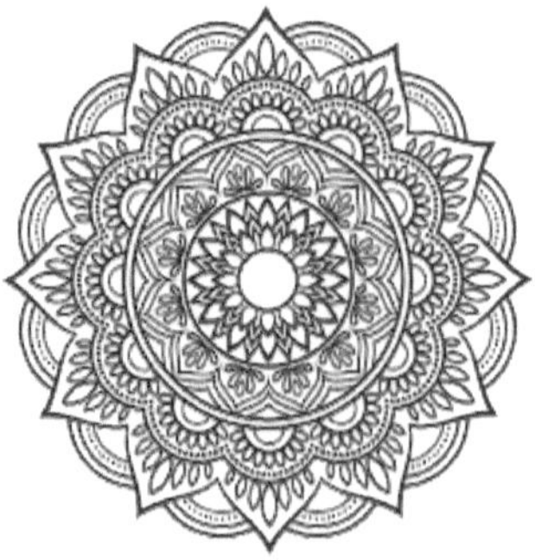
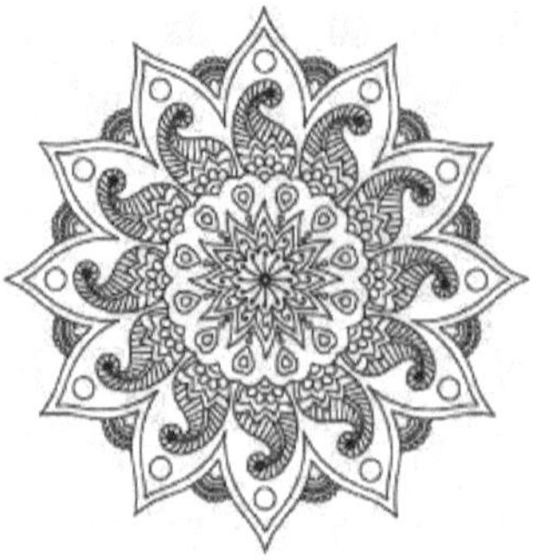

Deepavali / Diwali Celebrations

Deepavali comes from two words, "Deepam" and "Oli" which means the effulgence of light. In some parts of India and abroad, it is shortened to *Diwali*. Diwali is one of the many of the great Hindu festivals. It is the festival of lights, and has both the tradition of Thanksgiving and Christmas. We thank God on this day and share goodwill with fellow human beings.

Diwali is celebrated in memory of many different stories which all signify the victory of good over evil. For example, in Northern India, Hindus celebrate Diwali for God Rama killing Ravana and in Southern India, God Krishna killed Narakasura, and in Eastern India to honour Goddess Kali destroying Bakasura. Today all over the world we celebrate Diwali to signify good conquering evil.

Diwali falls in late October or early November. It falls on the darkest night of the year. In Hindu philosophy darkness is compared to ignorance and lighting the lamp has significance of dispelling ignorance and gaining knowledge. Whenever Hindus pray or perform any rituals they light an oil lamp (*Deepam*) first to signify the quest for knowledge and enlightenment.

On the day of Diwali, the whole family wakes up early, bathes and wears new clothes and ornaments. A breakfast follows the prayers. At night every home is lit with little lamps to attract the blessings of the Goddess of wealth, *Lakshmi* and Lakshmi pooja is performed. People go and pay respects to elders and exchange gifts and sweets. They try to forget old grudges. Businessmen bless their offices by performing Lakshmi pooja. They invoke Goddess Lakshmi to bless their new account books.

Our history is more than five thousand years old and still it promotes everlasting social and practical values of sharing, caring, forgiving and loving sentiments.

(In ancient times it was easy to distinguish good and evil, gods (*devas*) and demons. Now we have so many social injustices like drugs, prejudices and violence to face. Let us fight these underlying demons with illumination of our inner lights.)

Two Great Epics of Hinduism

The great epics of Hinduism are the *Ramayana* and the *Mahabharata*. They teach the people truth in an easy way and are appreciated and understood even by the uneducated. Hinduism accepts that the rules of society will change from time to time. The Ramayana and the Mahabharata have come down through the ages, enabling people of any time and age to carry within them wisdom of the *Upanishads* which are conveyed by these two epics. At the same time they are a means of guidance in one's life.

The Ramayana

The Ramayana was written by the great sage, *Rishi Valmiki*. The story is about Rama, (avatar of Lord Vishnu) born on earth to show the path of righteousness.

Dasaratha, the king of Ayodhya, had 4 sons Rama, born of his first wife Kausalya. Bharata, of his favourite queen, Kaikeyi, and Lakshmana and Shatrugan, born of his third wife, Sumitra.

Rama was banished to the forest for 14 years at the behest (command) of his step-mother, Kaikeyi. Dasaratha had earlier given her two boons. When the opportunity was right, she made Dasaratha send Rama away so that her son, Bharata could be king. Rama left with his wife Sita and his brother, Lakshmana. In the forest, Sita was abducted by the demon-king of Lanka called Ravana. Rama was helped by an army of monkeys and by Hanuman, who was the most loyal of them all. He fought and destroyed Ravana and managed to bring Sita back.

The epic is one to be remembered as it goes to show the qualities of all the characters as in the ideal queens, Kausalya and Sumitra, both soft-spoken but strong, who placed the prestige of their husband and king and the kingdom above the love for their sons. The two queens sent away their beloved sons so that King Dasaratha could keep his word. Rama being the ideal son agreed to go without any hesitation and was voluntarily accompanied by his younger brother, Lakshmana. It also shows the importance of spoken words-SATHYA, and the need to uphold DHARMA; these differentiate man from animal and raises him to Divine stature.

(This is only a brief outline of the Ramayana which conveys to mankind the great Human Values of TRUTH and RIGHTEOUSNESS - SATHYA and DHARMA)

Rama, Sita, Lakshmana and Hanuman

The Mahabharata

The *Mahabharata* was compiled by *Sage Vyasa*. It revolves around the Great War between two princely families, the righteous five *Pandava* brothers and their evil cousins, the hundred *Kauravas*. The main character is Lord Krishna (Avatar of Lord Vishnu.)

Arjuna, a great warrior was the General who led the battle. He belonged to the Pandava brothers. At the battlefield, the enemies he saw on the other side were his cousins, uncles and granduncles. So close was the relationship, that he refused to fight with them. Krishna, who acts as his charioteer, advises him on the importance of his *dharma* (duty), that he, Arjuna, a warrior must fight for righteousness. The Kauravas, who represented evil, must be destroyed so as to restore righteousness and harmony in the land.

The advise which Lord Krishna gave to Arjuna during the great Mahabharata War, at Kurukshetra, became a teaching which is called the *Bhagavad Gita* (song of the God). Here the Kaurava brothers represent worldly attachments which we have to fight against. In this epic, Lord Krishna emphasises the paths of Bhakti (devotion) and action without desire and without any attachment to the fruits or results of one's actions. The duty of an ideal man is to set right the wrongs in society. Therefore from the Mahabharata, both men and women, the rich and the poor, are able to learn the rules and codes of ideal conduct.

Krishna's advice to Arjuna

A Hindu Marriage - Saptapadi - The Marriage Vows

Significance:

The sacred fire represents the eternal cosmic energy (God). The groom and bride take seven steps around this cosmic energy and exchange their marriage vows with each other, experiencing a spiritual union in God. The vows being nourishment, moral and strength, chastity, happiness in parenthood, commitment, cherishment, eternal friendship, respect and love.

Step 1

Groom: My beloved, our love starts by your walking this step with me. You will offer me nourishment and be helpful in everyway, in turn, will cherish and provide for you and the family's welfare and happiness.

Bride: My humble submission to you my Lord is that you have entrusted me with the responsibility of our home, nourishment and finance. I promise you that I will carry out these responsibilities entrusted to me to the best of my ability.

Step 2

Groom: My beloved now, that you have walked the 2nd step with me, fill my heart with strength and courage and together we will protect our family and home.

Bride: With this second step, I pledge to protect our family and please you with sweet words. In your grief I shall bring solace and rejoice in your joy so that we work a harmonious relationship.

Step 3

Groom: Now you have walked 3 steps with me, I shall only look upon you as my wife and by virtue of this our family will prosper.

Bride: My Lord, I will love you with single mindedness.

Step 4

Groom: My Beloved, when you walk these steps with me, you bring great blessings, auspiciousness and sacredness into my life. May we also be blessed with healthy and noble children.

Bride: I will decorate you with flowers, garlands, and ornaments and anoint you with fragrant sandalwood pastes and perfumes. Also I will serve you and please you in every way I can.

Step 5

Groom: My beloved, now that you have walked five steps with me, you enrich my life. May God bless us and our loved ones and may we be a source of joy to them.

Bride: My Lord, as I take this 5th step, I am honoured to be chosen to share your life. Your love I will return with trust and honour whilst carrying your wishes.

Step 6

Groom: My beloved, you fill my heart with happiness by walking these six steps with me. May you continue to fill my heart with this same joy and peace from time to time.

Bride: My Lord, in all acts of righteousness, in material prosperity, in every form of enjoyment and divine acts, I promise you I shall participate and always be with you.

Step 7

Groom: My beloved, as you walk these seven steps with me our friendship and love becomes eternal. We have experienced spiritual union, with the Cosmic Energy as our witness. I offer you myself and a accept you completely as mine. Our union is for all time.

Bride: My Lord, as per the law of the Supreme Cosmic Energy and the Holy Scriptures, I have become your wife. Whatever promises we have exchanged, we have spoken with pure minds and hearts. We will be truthful in all matters, love, honour and respect each other for all time.

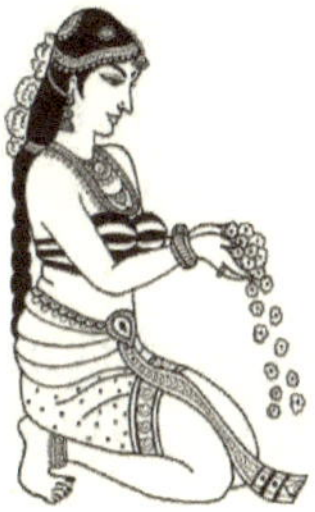

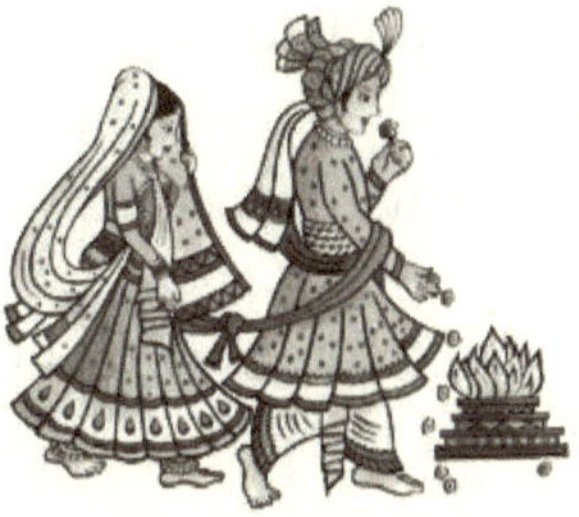

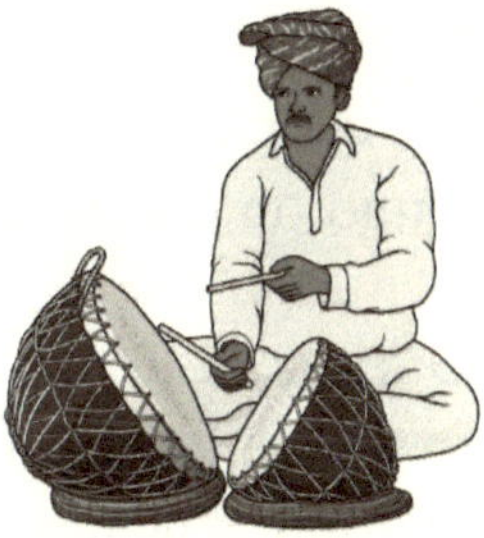

The Search For Peace

The word *peace* is used commonly and widely, and is the subject of interest for the entire universe. In spirituality, peace is mentioned all the time. Everything revolves around being at peace and keeping peace. Thus, it is important to understand the term, peace.

What is peace? Peace is *harmony* and *calmness*. Peace is *patience* and *understanding*. Peace is *tranquility* and *serenity*. To gain peace, one need not search for peace, as it is not in the exterior world. Peace resides within oneself, and to recognize it, turning introvert will assist one in identifying. Most folks try very hard in finding peace in worldly materials and peaceful localities. In true fact, one is not able to achieve that, for worldly materials and serene localities does not provide any peace or happiness, it is merely an indulgence. You may obtain peace and happiness in these forms only for a short period of time, but then, remember, it is not permanent. Such joy is only found on the surface and will phase out very hastily.

One may ask how to search for peace? The question is not to search, but rather "how to be at peace". Without peace of mind, it would deem difficult to function rationally and wisely. Only when there is spiritual knowledge and action, there is peace, victory, sound and glory. One needs to go to a stage of contemplation, and to start reasoning things out. Everything that goes on, everything that is being said or done must have a reason. All the pros and cons must be weighed. All the whys and musts must be checked. This is contemplation. There is a check on all thoughts and screening of actions. As each and everyone have his or her own nature it thus has its own tendency, making everyone different from the other. One must recognize its nature and carefully analyze. Life is about investigating, and adopting good nature. Acquiring good ways are credit points. Adopt and develop a sense of simplicity. The term simplicity is merely *acceptance*, where there are no traces of fussing, complaining or grumbling whatsoever. Expectations of any type hardly exist. There are certain reasons why people are not able to remain at peace. Such are the people who only want to belong in their comfort zone. They are too engrossed in the materialistic field. Always acquiring and taking only. They have no spirit of sacrifice and are always looking for the easy way out.

There is also a sense of uncertainty that when there isn't a form or an object, one is unable to *obtain* or *utilize* for pleasure. So they indulge in the material world as it has a form. In other words, spirituality does not have a form as it is not visible, it is just knowledge of the Self!

Another good example is, Nature. Nature is supplying us with most fundamental needs, but yet, we do not enquire nor appreciate. The sun shines throughout the day and the rain provides us with water and freshness. The breeze provides us with cool air and the moon shines during the dark. These are the essentials that are being provided throughout our lifetime, do not enjoy them blindly.

To be at peace, it *reflects the Self*. If one is doing good, you don't need another to certify or endorse it. Do not be elated or dejected when someone passes a comment or a remark. These remarks will not change anything, for you ought to know yourself at best. Nothing else matters, but you. Be steadfast and composed at all times. Do not look for the end fruits of success or its appreciation. The beauty is doing one's best of his ability that matters. This can be applied in all experiences.

When there is no feeling of being stretched, no fussing, no grumbling and no existence of pressure, the Self returns to its original state. The Self is at peace. It is just a matter of accepting rather than expecting as it could lead to a bundle of unhappiness that comes along. No individual should look for materials in a form for pleasure and comfort. But, in actual truth, knowledge is what is required.

To maintain the order of peace, one should eliminate *ego*. We cannot use ego to erase ego. The mind has to be dedicated to the self. One has to have realistic ideals. They must go beyond self-centredness. This is through sacrifice.

Why is it that some get onto spiritual path and the rest are not able to and live a routine existence? This solely depends on the individual. If a person desires to learn, he will learn and move forward in life. The other is merely dull and indolent and due to this non interest in spirituality, will not be able to develop a spirit of enthusiasm and will not enquire of what goes on around. They are oblivious to the surroundings and are just glued to their small way of thinking and doing things. There is no element of interest shown for self development. Also importantly required, is sheer discipline. One must not be victimised with all vicious desires that are undesirable. This would lead to sufferings.

To be at peace, the presence and substance of *ill feelings* in an individual must be eliminated as this would eventually lead to destruction. Do not adopt a habit of passing a *judgement* or a *remark* on others without first understanding the situation. Judgements and remarks are in fact sometimes not necessary. Ill feelings will emerge and at times produce space to retaliate at the spur of the moment. This would pave the way for many to become upset. To keep under control, [try and understand the pattern of each individual and act accordingly. We should not expect them to be the way we like them to be. Thus, do not roam freely and simply do not trail blindly and mechanically. As one cannot find comfort in a solitary place, than find a solitary time and proceed.

What Are Desires

What are *desires* and why it is important to keep them under control? What it takes to work towards having less desire? If desires exist, is it alright to fulfill them? These are questions that are repeatedly being asked.

Desires are *fleeting objects* that infest the Mind. Desires are a stream of thoughts flowing towards an object. Desires are like bacteria, if not checked, they multiply very quickly. These desires come to the mind as thoughts, and thus actions are produced thereafter.

Every desire needs to be checked. It is better to drop what is unnecessary; for it holds responsible for all mental agitation of life. There must be self-control. This means that one should not plunge into anything without enquiring. It is better to enhance the self to abstain from desires and remain self-contented. This must come with an attitude of willingness to perform. Do not self deny, but to a stand of willingness. To *self deny* does not make sense as it would pave the way in creating frustrations and forbid one to indulge.

The *willingness* to avoid must be present so that even though the desire is not realized there is no longer a thought left in the mind. The desire has been erased totally.

When a desire is fulfilled, it will lead one to yearn for more and more. There is no end to acquiring. Cravings become deeper and one lead to seek greater enjoyment. This is merely treading towards greediness. And when greed is fed with more acquisition and enjoyment, arrogance develops in the Self. For example, the Self becomes arrogant and envious with anyone whom comes in contact. There is no such thing of level headedness.

When a desire exists in the mind, do not put force to obtain without proper means and beyond one's capability. This will prove to be futile. There must not be any pressure upon the Self to obtain. Thus, it is always good to check if it is within one's mean to obtain.

What would happen when a desire is *unfulfilled*? When the aim to desire of obtaining has failed or is unfulfilled, the self would go all out to obtain by whatever deems fit, whether it is the proper way or otherwise. There is no end to the list of cravings and attainment. Once the desire is not accomplished, the Self will start to lose control over itself. The following states what happens when a desire is unfulfilled.

When thoughts come to the mind, they are desires. When desires are not accomplished, the self becomes agitated and disoriented. One becomes angry and starts to lose control of everything. He or she forgets what is right and what is wrong, what is good or what is bad. The person is infuriated and is unable to think rationally, and starts to forget all obligations and relationships and thus, tantamount to lost of memory. In the process, his personality will perish and gives the individual a negative image. This would than lead to *disaster* as the desire had not been acquired. Thus, one would go into a process of mental agitation and also brings about difficulties to others who are in contact.

Agitations related to *unfulfilled desires* will result in loss of concentration, calmness, clarity of thought, discontentment and unable to think rationally. One will tend to become selfish and the definition for selfish is catering to oneself only. It is indeed a must to inculcate a sense of *unselfishness* as it caters to accommodate everyone alike.

To eliminate the process of being unhappy, angry and misery, <u>it is required to locate the underlying desire and remove it</u>. Do not allow desire to fulfill the void and fill with worldly materials and pleasures.

Desires must be kept under tight scrutiny and constantly checked, otherwise there is no end to unnecessary acquiring. When a thought reaches an object, the Self should analyze, discriminate, judge, accept or reject. Do not allow it to flow freely and be strengthened.

The doer has to choose the desired action and act accordingly. There is no one who can lure the self, other than the Self. The weak self is overcome with such emotions, desires or cravings that it promotes them to act. This mere poor performance is the doing of a weak person with poor intellect. The intellect seems to have no control over the mind and the mind is now free to dwell on whatever comes. There seems to be no effort of judging or discrimination from right or wrong. Things are done in an undesired manner thus attributing to the decay of action, deeds and thoughts.

The Lotus Flower – Symbol of Purity

Vegetarianism

These days *vegetarianism* is gaining fast popularity amongst the masses and *vegetarians* are known to be all over the world. A vegetarian diet is considered much healthier than consuming meat.

There are a good number of people who have been vegetarians ever since they were born. This may be linked to a religious factor, a belief that killing of animals for meat is incorrect or there are those who are against the usage of animal products and manufacture.

There are amongst many people as well, who have been consuming meat for many years and in the long run, have decided to change their diet and to embrace vegetarianism. And of course there are those whom had never tasted meat all their lives suddenly decide to eat meat. It could be a decision made at the spur of the moment or a change of lifestyle, reasons only known best to them. As the years go by, it has become vary that being a vegetarian helps maintain a healthy life. With the recent outbreaks of diseases deriving from animals, there seems to be some awareness that one is likely to be afflicted with some form of sickness.

Animals being animals, do have their liberty to live. As intelligent human beings, the killing of animals for their meat and skin is sheer pleasure for the tongue and physical outlook. Do not contribute to the killings and sufferings of animals. For those who choose to lead a spiritual life, it deems necessary to be a vegetarian. This is the way to stride onto spiritual path. The aspirant has to understand the importance of *'why be a vegetarian'* and that meat must not be consumed. This is necessary as it cleanses the body system and mind. It paves the way and keeps the conscious clear from playing any part of the killings of animals and consuming its meat for pleasure. *Killing in the spiritual field is considered wrong. Everyone knows and says aloud that animals are the Creations of the Almighty, and yet, on the other hand, animals are killed for their meat. Many a times, killed in an atrocious manner. This is merely a double standard of living. How can anyone kill when we say that "we love the Almighty"; whilst <u>severing</u> and <u>torturing</u> His Creation. This is absurdity at its highest. One must stop and ponder if this practice is correct or mere ignorance.*

Some facts about animals. The biggest and strongest land animal is the elephant. It is a *herbivorous*, meaning vegetarian. It has a calm and composed nature. The cow is a picture of *grace* and *beauty*, eating only grass and water as its diet, but has the strength to plough the fields for the farmers. The giraffe is very tall and lives on a vegetarian diet. A picture of *peace*.

Here are some other animals that are vegetarian and friendly to mankind. They include the, horse, rabbit, deer, rhinoceros, buffalo, hippopotamus and camel. etc

Meditation

Meditation is an effort directed to the self to aim for the highest ideal, which is self-realization. One has to be constant and fixed in meditation. That fixation or effort is called *faith*. Meditation is a scientific technique which helps exhaust desires and unnecessary thoughts that is present in the mind. The self must be free from all evil thoughts and deeds. It is the highest spiritual practice and to meditate, it requires a calm mind. The fleeting mind and the senses must be kept under control at all times. An agitated mind is most unlikely for meditation and cannot be brought to single-pointedness.

To meditate, the individual must at least try and release whatever agitation that is present in the mind. This will help in being focused and concentrated.

Made in United States
Troutdale, OR
07/09/2023